'Master-Minding NLP Ad Copy That Really Sells Like Billy-O!'

FOUR BANANAS ON AN UPSIDE-DOWN TREE!

by Russell Webster

RUSSELL WEBSTER

A RETIRE EARLY PRODUCTION

Here is an outstanding fact.

Only 1% of the population of the modern world will ever be totally financially independent at retirement age!!

Another, rather more worrying, fact is that 95% of the same populations will require some State help at the same age.

Why is that?

The reasons are numerous: from illness to laziness. Yet if we had to pick just one reason it would be that the vast majority of people surround themselves with the wrong influences – the wrong environment.

In this instance the `wrong environment' is the people you surround yourself with, the TV you watch, the books you read.
If, however, you mix with successful people you will gradually learn all of habits they have, from setting goals to taking the right kind of actions. You will also find that opportunities start to come your way.

In the absence of such people to bounce off then you simply MUST devour as many books, audio books, videos as you possibly can. We can help you with this!

We have made our books bite sized so that you can read them quickly and take the main points out of them. Our audio books are a great way to fill your mind with great information whilst you are travelling, and our Videoliminals are simply ground-breaking!

More about our exciting range of products at the end of this book.

Also please visit our website -

www.retireearlyproductions.com

info@retireearlyproductions.com

It only takes one small piece of information to totally change your whole life!

The Retire Early Team

ABOUT THE AUTHOR

Russell Webster describes himself as an entrepreneurial version of Stephen Fry. He is an eclectic creator of new ideas and new concepts, widely published as an audio book writer and narrator, and an accomplished speaker.

In the late 1980s his first venture was to conceive, design and construct one of the UK's recording studios – The Slaughterhouse, which gained huge notoriety for recording the first Happy Monday gold album and visitors such as Brian May from Queen.

Music always was and still is one of his great passions, along with a voracious appetite for knowledge in all fields of psychology from Freud and Jung right up to Bandler and Grinder who pioneered NLP (Neuro Linguistic Programming).

After losing the studio in a fire Russell took time out to write his own music and become qualified in NLP.

He then pioneered a new type of audio book, of which he wrote several, narrated them himself AND added music underneath the spoken word. This was a great success and he has sold hundreds of thousands worldwide. They still sell just as well today.

Strangely enough it was when he finally wrote Seven Secrets (along with creating a musical score for it with a friend) he learned why he was only being moderately successful and made a huge change in his life by moving to London and launching a new business in the training field.

By applying his own principles to his new business he very quickly became wealthy. Then, when his marriage failed, he let the whole thing go so that he could be near his children.

After a topsy-turvy few years (to put it mildly) he spent two years writing his first actual book – SNAFU, which stands for Situation Normal All F***** Up. Although it was written as a novel it is quite a deep book. It delves into both success and failure and is best read by people who want to become counsellors or therapists. You do also find out a lot more about Russell, and the impact his childhood had on him. And on others.

Then, recently, he noticed that something really was, in his mind, heralding the total breakdown of the traditional family – console games and apps. His own children could hardly tear themselves away from their iPhones, iPods, iPads, and X-Box game long enough to say hello to him. He looked around him and found that this was widespread - so many children were no longer communicating with their parents in the way that children used to.

So, in 2015 he set about creating a board game. Yes, a traditional board game called THE FAMILY GAME - with Brian Brain's National Curriculum.

It is live and available now on Amazon and, fortuitously, it brought him together with a long-standing friend, Peter Aldred. Peter not only loved the game but also loved all of Russell's audio creations.

A partnership was formed in 2016. That partnership is called Retire Early Productions. As well as turning quite a few of Russell's audio books into 'real' books Peter and he came up with an exciting and ground breaking new concept called Videoliminals – combination of the spoken word, relaxing music and video.

You cannot keep a creative person quiet for long!

"In time of profound change the learners inherit the earth while the learned find themselves beautifully equipped to deal with the world that no longer exists..."

AL

Rogers

ABOUT THIS BOOK

In this book you will learn about some of the fundamental criteria for writing successful advertising copy. If you are new to the concept of advertising then you will find this book invaluable. If you are a seasoned advertiser then this book will offer you a more cutting edge approach to the concept of advertising.

The principles in this book are based upon years of research, sound common sense, practical experience and practical applied psychologies such as Neuro Linguistic Programming (NLP). Furthermore, you can apply these principles straight away to make a significant difference in the effectiveness of your advertising: whatever medium you are using to advertise.

My name is Russell Webster, and I shall be guiding you through this book, which is designed as an introduction to the need to apply a set formula to your advertising. I have to warn you that some things, some sentences, will make me sound like a deranged lunatic. They will not make sense to you, but that is kind of the point. So just ignore them OR GO WITH THE FLOW.

They are just Eriksonian linguistics. HE WAS A GENIOUS! HE WAS THE ULTIMATE MASTER OF SUBLIMINAL AUTIO SUGGESTION WHO CONFUSED THE CONSCIOUS MIND AND THEN PLANTED SUBLIMINAL (AUTO SUGGESTIVE) MESSAGES IN HIS PATIENTS.

WRITING STUNNING ADVERTISING COPY WITH NLP

RUSSELL WEBSTER

FOREWORD

It seems strange to think that this is now about to become a `real' book. How much has changed in the 15 years since I wrote it as an audio book?

What would I change in the script?

The answer is NOTHING!

Well, not quite. I had to change the title. The previous title was literally too close to the bone!

It worked though.

James Russell Webb

RUSSELL WEBSTER

ACKNOWLEDGMENTS

To my brother Brad, who, over the years, has consistently helped me with proof-reading, editing and formatting.

WRITING STUNNING ADVERTISING COPY WITH NLP

DEDICATION

I dedicate this book to the child that still resides in most of us. We all had such great dreams but most of us lacked the knowledge or drive to fulfil those dreams.

Yet, it is never too late!

WRITING STUNNING ADVERTISING COPY WITH NLP

CONTENTS

There are also two appendices. The first is bonus advice from great copywriters. The second is A SHORT INTRODUCTION TO NLP.

CHAPTER ONE

So, my work colleague said to me "how do you write great ad copy?"

"Four bananas on an upside down tree." I said.

He stopped dead in his tracks and said, "Do what?" He looked awfully confused.

"Exactly", I said. "The first thing you must do is stop people dead in their tracks, break their current thought patterns and get them to pay attention to your advert. Whether you are advertising above the line such as off-the-page or on TV or below the line with something like mailshots you have to get the headline line to open their minds and make them receptive. The same applies to internet marketing too, if not more so."

"Then what?" he asked

"You have to attempt to anticipate what underlying value someone might attach to having your product or service. Anticipate what might be their true motivation."

"We are talking about benefits here" he said.

"In a way" I said "but the word benefit is a little fluffy, very non-specific, and very open to the wrong interpretation. It goes deeper than that"

"Okay, then what?" he asked.

"You then have to create a reason to act within a given timescale and offer an easy mechanism for them to respond to your advert"

"What exactly does that mean" he enquired.

"Well it's no good getting someone to the stage of simply wanting your product or service, tearing out the ad or mentally filing an interest.   You have to attach a sense of urgency and also make it incredibly easy for them to then buy your product or service."

All will be explained in the coming pages, and, as you listen carefully, you will realise that your business could explode over the next few months, with all of the things that may mean to you and your family and your lifestyle when you start to use this technique tonight, tomorrow and every day thereafter.

CHAPTER TWO

Have you ever sat through the commercial break and not even noticed a single advert. Have you ever reached for the remote control during the same break?

Have you ever sat watching the adverts on TV, barely paying attention, when a certain commercial caused you to focus a little more and pay some attention?

Have you also noticed that you invariably did nothing about it the following day, or week or month?

Have you ever cut an advert out of the paper and meant to respond to it, but never did?

Do you ever read a newspaper and scan the headline banners to decide which articles you are going to read?

Did you know that sex or sexy pictures attract more people's attention than anything else? Of course you did.

Have you ever written advertising copy that simply failed to pull in the results that you had hoped for or expected?

Have you ever wished that you could design adverts that really worked?

I am going to make the assumption that you have already written advertising copy, or are about to, and have wondered - and are wondering - how to make your advertising more effective. This short book will give you a working formula to do exactly that. If you are about to advertise for the first time then this slim volume should save you a fortune.

Primarily the information here is aimed at those people writing off-the-page adverts, flyers inserts or mail order copy. However the same basic rules apply to all other forms of advertising, including television commercials, where, although there are huge advantages such as adding music, movement and appealing to all three primary senses, many advertisers still go about the job in an old-fashioned way. And, obviously the internet.

If you were sensible you will have used a formula to design your advert. The most common of these is AIDA, A. I. D. A.

A stands for Attention.

I stands for Interest.

D stands for Desire.

And the final A stands for Action.

Aida is crude, but far more effective than going blind, as many people do. If you can grab someone's attention, create an interest in your product or service, build up the desire and then give your potential customer a reason to take action then you will have the basis of an effective advert.

The chances are though that whilst writing the copy, having come up with your attention grabbing headline and building in all of the things that YOU think will be of interest and be desirable to a potential customer, it will become far too busy.

And then, due to budget constraints, it is likely that you will end up with an advert that is a jumbled mess and one which is crammed into too small a space. The headline, which started quite large, will probably shrink into insignificance to make way for other information; and your advert will be all but useless. It will become the proverbial waste of time and definitely a waste of money.

Too much information always has the opposite effect to what was intended. One of the golden rules about advertising is that: **LESS IS MORE**. Just as a good music producer will look to create a gap in the music to create effect and retain interest a bad one will try and fill that same gap and the result will be unpleasant to the ears.

Complex product descriptions or irrelevant Company information is normally a waste of valuable space. How do you think this advert might work?

Sex is free
With the ABC
Call 0300 sex!
That's 0300 sex!
Now.
This offer lasts for only one hour.

CHAPTER THREE

There are many books available on advertising and they are packed with ideas and knowledge that you can pull into a basic framework such as AIDA.

However, Aida is becoming a little geriatric, old fashioned and out of date. Aida does not function quite as well as it used to. It is just a little woolly or non- specific and in the economic climate of today and tomorrow, more precise, cutting edge methods are needed if you are to survive and prosper, or, even better, get exceptional results.

So, who are you trying to sell your product or service to? Dumb question? Maybe, maybe not.

People, is of course the correct answer. But it's not a very specific answer is it? Should you try to sell socks to people's feet or gloves to people's hands? Do hands or feet make decisions?

HANDY GLOVES ARE MADE OF SPECIAL FIBRES AND WILL MAKE YOUR HANDS FEEL JUST GREAT ALL YEAR ROUND.

On a scale of one to ten how do you feel about buying a pair of our gloves? Are your hands excited? Probably not.

Can you remember a time when *YOU WERE REALLY INTERESTED IN LEARNING SOMETHING NEW?*

Can you *NOW* remember a time when you felt particularly uncomfortable or even upset about something?

Can you remember being outdoors, in winter and very cold?

If you can't then just pretend you can. Test your acting skills here and really get fully into this, as if you were able to feel every emotion.

Imagine you are in a crowd of people, possibly watching some event. The temperature is sub-zero and, as the bitter wind is driving into your face, your feet have chilblains and you can no longer feel your hands. You notice people leaving, because they can't stand it anymore. As each person leaves your hands become even colder and you feel more and more miserable.

And then there is only one person left. That person is also incredibly attractive, and for some reasons unbeknown to you he or she seems remarkably cheerful, happy, content and warm. As you think this you feel a twinge of jealousy. What does he or she know that you don't? What have they got that you have not.

Then, as you too finally give up and walk back to the car and try to get your car keys out you realise that you have lost so much feeling in your hands and fingers that you can't even fish them out of your pocket. As you look up and notice the one remaining vehicle in the car park, obviously belonging to the person who stayed, you notice the signwriting on his van. It says:

LIFE SEEMS SO MUCH BETTER AND MORE EXCITING WITH WARM HANDS!
HANDYGLOVES WILL KEEP YOUR HANDS WARM AND PUT A CHEESY GRIN ON YOUR FACE WHEN OTHERS HAVE HAD TO TAKE THEIR TEDDY BEAR HOME.
It is the strangest phenomenon!

On a scale of one to ten how do you feel about handy gloves now? Hopefully you will feel somewhat stronger about our gloves now. If not, you have not participated properly or you are brain dead.

Would you like to live to a ripe old age? As you make up a small mental picture of handy gloves in your mind's eye do you remember being in love? Would you like to be extremely popular and well respected in all of your dealings with others? Would you like to be financially secure to the point whereby you could have virtually any possession you would like? A recent survey has shown that handy gloves have a peculiar ability to bring about a general sense of well-being, great feelings and prosperity.

On a scale of one to ten how do you feel about handy gloves now?

If you feel more strongly about our gloves *now* then that's great. Maybe gloves just are not your thing and that's okay too. I would however wager that from zero or one out of ten you increased your interest slightly, even with an unglamorous subject or product like gloves. If you started at one and got to two then that's a doubling up of effectiveness in your receptivity. It will have happened because you have associated feelings to the product.

What is important is to realise one fundamentally important thing: Whatever your product or service is you are not selling it to people or parts of their body!

You are selling it to their control centre: the part that collates all information and decides how it makes them feel emotionally or logically: their brain or their mind.

I simply cannot emphasise this enough. You are appealing to the mind! The complex series of organs that controls every single organ, heartbeat, every foot, toe, hand, finger. The part of the body that regulates body temperature, thirst, hunger and sex drive. The most amazingly complex mass of protoplasm in the known universe. The one that weighs less than two percent of the body's total weight yet requires twenty percent of the body's' oxygen. IT is the part that makes all decisions about logic or about feelings.

To become a master advertiser you need to become a master of understanding the human brain or mind.

I am now going to map out an advertising framework that is more advanced than Aida. It draws upon the laws of psychology and advanced psychologies such as Neuro Linguistic Programming, which is the cutting edge understanding of how human beings interpret and process information and eventually therefore make the decisions that you want them to make.

CHAPTER FOUR

Aida's got a pussy.

The secret of writing hugely successful adverts lies in Aida's pussy. Whoops!!

> AUTHOR'S NOTE – the original audio version of this book had quite an outrageous title and it sure as hell got people's attention – STROKING AIDA'S PUSSY!

HOWEVER, THE PRINCIPLE WAS TOTALLY CORRECT.   THE PRINCIPLE ALSO STANDS AS IT WAS ALSO USED AS THE PRE-CURSER TO AN ACRONYM: PURR

So, back to the plot.

If you can stroke and make Aida's pussy purr then he or she will eat out of your hand.

To help you remember this framework I am going to use the word *PURR* as an acronym to help remind you of the four stages of the process.

P stands for pattern interrupt.

Everyone has a mass of thought patterns going through their brains at any one given moment in time: a myriad of different thought processes. You do right now. Some of them are dominant and occupy pride of place where others are tucked away a little. Certain events or other thoughts may cause you to change thought patterns for a while but the dominant thought pattern will quickly return.

To write headline copy that is effective you have to interrupt all those patterns of thought.

It's a more sophisticated approach than simply trying to grab people's attention, as what works for one person, or maybe even all three of the sexes, does not necessarily work for another one down and three up when one man's meat is another man's bra. Especially when your pen runs out of white ink at the pussycat flying down upside.

Confused?

Then maybe I have interrupted your pattern sufficiently enough to command your undivided attention for just one moment...

...which of course makes all of the difference? It's the difference that makes the difference. Whether I can retain your attention depends totally upon what you might achieve for *yourself*, your *company* or your *family* by listening carefully. How many extra holidays might you be able to take? How much more free time might you have? How much longer might you live?

This bit is a bit heavy

Bringing this down to a scientific level people basically have four types of patterns going on in their heads. Two of them are at a conscious level and two of them are at a level below the conscious.

Your *dominant conscious patterns* are those things that are currently right at the front of your thinking. Normally they are just one or two things: immediate thought patterns. It could be something you must get done to justify your immediate existence:

the job at hand, the phone call you need to make, someone who has just annoyed you, the business expansion plan you are writing. Whatever it is these thought patterns are those that dominate your brain at any given time. Many people don't notice anything else going on around them when they are zoned in on a particularly compelling dominant thought pattern. You walk past and they don't even see you. You say something and they don't listen. You think they are rude or ignorant. Maybe you have done the same thing and found yourself apologising... "Sorry I was miles away."

If you make the assumption that everyone that you are trying to advertise to is ignorant, miles away or on a different planet then you might start to realise that it is no easy task that you face.

Next comes your *unresolved conscious patterns*. These are all of those things that have to be done at some stage, either during the course of the next hour or two, day or so, week, month or so or during your lifetime.

They are like open files that clutter up the desk or the mental desk: your brain. Calls you must make or return, reports to be written, shopping to be done, anniversary cards to be bought, credit cards to pay off, car to get serviced, relations to visit, boss to appease and so on. I am sure you could add to the list... These unresolved thought patterns are never far away from the surface and occasionally pop up into your mind and become the dominant pattern of the moment.

As you now think of some of those unresolved issues in your work life or in your private life you might notice that you are not actually listening to this audio as carefully as you were. Maybe another thought pattern has become dominant.

That's why seventeen is and always will be the most important number in your life!

Because then you have *emotional sub-conscious patterns*. These are your emotional agendas, the things that are important to you in your life. They are the things that you value strongly and care deeply about. The things that you really believe in and that are important to you on a deeper level: maybe your partner and your family. They also include your own self-indulgences, personal desires and wishes. The area of your brain that houses these thoughts is by far the most complex.

It keeps psychologists in business. It is the centre of your emotional being and, what is incredibly important to know is that every decision of any importance you make is firstly ratified or checked out by this part of your brain. It is the ecology centre of your brain. It is the area where consequence, value and meaning take place.

Every time you make a decision this part of your brain checks out whether it fits in with what you value in life.

If some of your core values were safety, and being close to your partner and family and someone tried to sell you on the concept of a new job that offered you three times the income you presently have, yet meant that you would spend half the year away from home and also had some danger attached to it then this part of your brain would click in and most probably over-ride the pleasant aspects of a mammoth income.

Emotional sub-conscious thought patterns are powerful. When someone is in love these thought patterns seem to over-ride virtually all else. If someone dear to you dies these emotions can often consume you. The same often happens when a relationship breaks up.

These thought patterns, which operate at a level below the conscious, also have a hand in controlling innate drives such as thirst hunger and sex.

The important thing to remember here is that this is the part of the human brain, of people, that you must sell your product to. It is the decision maker. It is this area that you must get into to be hugely effective with your advertising. Someone's emotional sub-conscious thought patterns.

Finally, you have *primal sub-conscious patterns,* which operate at a very deep level. These patterns govern your survival: your need to live and your need for warmth and shelter and only come to the fore when any of these are under threat. One could argue that appealing to these primal or primitive emotions is crossing a certain line and should not be used. That is a decision only you can make. It is important to realise how important they can be in understanding the human brain or mind. If there were suddenly an impending worlwide shortage of food, maybe through threat of nuclear war, then you would not even have to advertise. Your shop would be stripped bare within a short space of time. Imagine that you could write copy that would have that effect.

When you start to grasp the concepts of how the human brain works you will start to think about your advertising more carefully and will get better results.

CHAPTER FIVE

This book is occupying a pattern in your mind. Every time you have a thought process or you think of something you must do, a new pattern opens: a little like opening a drawer and pulling a file out. For the pattern to close it must have an outcome or finality to it.

What happens for most people is that the mental office has loads of open files in it? Their brains are busily whirring away with all sorts of weird and wonderful thought processes. If you stop and think about it you may know exactly what your current and immediate task is, but the chances are that there are hundreds of other unresolved issues. Work issues, family issues, hobby issues, hidden agendas etcetera. These are open patterns buzzing around in your head: many of which you are, possibly, totally unaware of.

As you think about a time, maybe even now, when your head was spinning with so many different thought processes, open patterns, unresolved issues, incomplete dealings, and forthcoming events that you had to plan for that your brain was like a battle zone, then how receptive are you to someone advertising their product? I would suggest not very.

To a lesser or greater degree this is exactly what is going through people's minds most of the time.

Have you noticed how some people hardly seem to be listening when you are talking to them or people who interrupt you? How would you like to have to advertise your product or service to a world made up of people like that?

WRITING STUNNING ADVERTISING COPY WITH NLP

It is a fundamental starting point when advertising your product or service to assume that everyone is too busily wrapped up in their own thoughts to really pay much time or any attention whatsoever to your advert. You have to be damned cunning to get them to stop and take notice.

There's a battle going on in most people's minds and the only ways to get someone to sit bolt upright and pay attention are to either drop a bomb or create confusion. You could advertise something that someone has been meaning to buy for weeks but the ad doesn't really register.

You need to totally interrupt their thinking or pattern, and replace it with a new pattern that is more interesting, appealing, confusing or compelling than the others. Preferably one that hits at the heart of their emotions, or emotional sub-conscious thought patterns. In other words, your ad must create their undivided attention.

Can you remember a time when you were having a blazing row with someone? If not, then just pretend that you can. And it is a major issue.

In the midst of the argument, just as things are getting more heated a fire-engine comes screaming up the drive, sirens blaring and lights flashing. The fire-engine pulls right up to the house; some of the firemen pile out and start unravelling the hose, whilst the others hoist up the ladders against the side of your house or apartment block.

Do you think that it might just interrupt the argument pattern? Incidentally, as mentioned in the title, if you find yourself genuinely having an argument and you want to get someone to stop and listen then just interrupt their pattern by saying something totally unrelated or bizarre. It always works.

"Seventeen times I've tried these shoes on tomorrow."

"What!! That's got nothing to do with what I am trying to tell you."

"I know, but seventeen times I have tried them on and my elbow is sore."

"What on earth are you on about?"

"Cream cakes."

"Cream cakes?"

Bingo, the pattern is broken. It always works.

If you were sat at home reading a book or watching television and suddenly there was a power failure it would suddenly command your undivided attention. That is an instant pattern interrupt.

Would you like to be able to write copy that would have that effect on virtually everyone?

If you were in a battlefield and a bomb dropped twenty yards away do you think that it might be equally as effective?

If you were having one of those boring conversations with someone and they suddenly started to unzip their trousers or skirt and take them off might that just interrupt your wandering mind?

CHAPTER SIX

Grabbing someone's attention is not quite strong enough. You have to find something; a headline that will cut through people's dominant thought patterns.

When a light bulb flickers it will normally wake you up from whatever thought pattern you are in at the time. Therefore, it does not have to be an earth-shattering headline.

Mild confusion is often as effective as anything! The minute the brain becomes confused it tends to give that issue and the following statement more pride of place. It is a technique I commonly used by the best hypnotherapists.

Typeface or font usage can play a role for you in achieving the same result. Just turning one letter around often works.

Clever usage of graphics can also be effective at interrupting thought patterns. We will go into more detail on methods in the follow up volume: nineteen bottles upside in a tree or advanced pussy stroking.

Understanding that thought patterns have a hierarchy will also assist you enormously. Remember the four types of pattern. *Dominant conscious, unresolved conscious, emotional sub-conscious and primal sub-conscious?* If you were busily going about your day to day routine and someone reminded you they were coming for dinner tonight to celebrate your partner's birthday, which you had, of course temporarily forgotten about, then that might become your dominant thought process for a short while.

If, ten minutes later someone rushed into the room and announced that the company was going bankrupt then that would interrupt your pattern again and become dominant. You might even become a little worried. The company also runs the savings plan that you have invested in for years and that is now at risk.

The effect of this on every aspect of your life and your family's life is potentially all-consuming in your thoughts. Your emotional sub-conscious agenda is suddenly your conscious agenda. What will it mean? Many of the things you value are suddenly threatened or at risk.

The words *worry* and *stress* might feature here.

Whilst you are considering this, and what to do about it, the phone rings. One of your children has been knocked down by a car and has been rushed into hospital. I am suggesting to you that that would then become your dominant thought pattern.

Your emotions would be over-riding all other thoughts.

As you get out of the car, and are running towards the hospital doors a gunman steps out and starts firing bullets into the air and screaming his head off. I suggest to you that your dominant thought pattern would instantly switch to that of survival and you would seek shelter.

Not a great day heh? However, the point is that thought patterns have priorities. The artform of writing excellent copy is to make your headline interrupt and then become your potential customer's dominant thought pattern. Appealing to the emotional or primal sub-conscious is going to have the greatest effect.

Using something from the next three parts of the acronym, as a headline grabber, can also be very effective in interrupting someone's pattern, and can kill two birds with one stone as well as saving space and being more minimalist.

CHAPTER SEVEN

Nobody, but nobody, buys a car because they want a car. Nobody buys a conservatory because they want a conservatory.

Nobody buys an investment or life policy because they want a piece of paper that says `policy' on it. Nobody buys advertising space because they covet advertising space. Nobody buys a computer because they want a box full of electronics and a free screen saver package.

They do however, buy solutions or consequence. What they do buy is what it does for them. What value it creates for them in their life or for their business. How it makes them feel. What value to themselves they associate with having your product or service. In other words, there is a hidden agenda or an underlying motive for purchasing anything.

U stands for underlying motive.

What will they become if they own your product?

What will their policy do for them when it matures? What feelings do they attach to that?

What will the computer help them to achieve and how will they then feel?

What's the payback in terms of personal satisfaction or gratification or in business terms?

People do things for the strangest reasons. Or do they?

WRITING STUNNING ADVERTISING COPY WITH NLP

In fact, people's reasons for doing can be categorised into what is known as metaprograms in Neuro Linguistic Programming.

To mention but a few: some people are more interested in what others think of them rather than what they think of themselves. They purchase solely on that basis.

Others are motivated by the pleasure of having, doing or owning something where others are motivated by the displeasure or pain of not having that same thing. If you assumed that fifty percent of the population were motivated by the displeasure of not having, then your advertising effort is instantly halved if you only address pleasurable reasons for owning your product or service.

They need to know what painful experiences thay might suffer as a result of not having your product or service.

Some people want to belong and be the same as others, yet some people strive to be different, and are totally motivated by that.

Therefore, there is a sorting process that has goes on in people's brains: often unbeknown to them.

What will others think of them? How will they feel about themselves? What will they be avoiding or what will they be gaining?

What fringe benefits might they receive?

How will they be different to others with your product or service?

Or how might it enable them to be the same?

What will happen in their lives as a result of having your product or service?

It is therefore very important to create an association with your advertising. *If* followed by *then.*

Professional TV advertisers understand this concept better than most. Buy these jeans and have more sex appeal. Buy her these chocolates and she will love you forever.

However, we are straying into the realms of TV advertising here where the advantage is overwhelming. They are able to appeal to all three of the major senses: sight, sound and feelings. They can get into your emotional patterns more easily, which is a powerful place to be.

They can use the powerful medium of music to enhance their advert and can also use communication to the full.

It might surprise you to know that research has proven that only 7% percent of human communication is attributable to the words you use: Hello.

38% percent is attributable to the intonation or voice inflection used; Helloooooo! And a massive 55% percent is body language.

Imagine an angry-looking teacher, his or her eyes are scrunched, they have a clenched fist, and their index finger is pointing at a certain pupil, which could be you, and then beckoning the said pupil to come to the front of the class. That is total communication, without a word being uttered. Do therefore remember to use effective imagery where you can and make up the missing gaps that TV advertsisers have.

The plot thickened and the gravy was ready to pour, and if I asked you to name a SCANDINAVIAN car that was built like a tank, but had a reputation for its level of protection and safety, what would it be.

The type of person who deliberately buys that particular make of car has almost certainly got an underlying motive of safety in mind.

CHAPTER EIGHT

If you take the word motivation and split it in two then it becomes a motive to take action. Motives are the things that you value and deem important. If *safety* has a high value for you this will override most other considerations. If high per*formance and sexy looks are an important value to you this is may not be the car for you.*

If you have successfully interrupted someone's thought pattern and you then proceed to bore them to tears with information that they can not relate to or perceive any value from then you will lose them quickly.

Selling the idea of whiteness simply does not do that much for most people. When crisp, clean white shirts have been linked with greater career enhancement and an almost uncontrollable sex appeal then that washing powder takes on a totally new appeal.

Tell them that they will become rich, successful, live longer, and be more attractive to the opposite sex, and generally be thought more highly of, by having your product or service and you are nearly there.

Warn them that they may be missing out on something and that if they do not have that powder others will think worse of them and that in general terms displeasurable things may be associated with not using your particular product.

In other words, you have to create a strong association to your product. If and then. If you have this, then you will that or become that. Or, if you don't use our product... then you will not.

The next step is to create a sense of urgency.

CHAPTER NINE

R stands for Reaction time.

Have you ever seen something advertised and thought 'oh yes I wouldn't mind one of those!' and made a decision to get one? But then a little time went by and you didn't get it at all or you bought a different brand?

Conversely have you seen or read an advert where the product appealed to you and where the advert stated quite definitely that if you don't get it before the end of the weekend then stocks will have run out or the sale will be over, and done something about it?

An action, as in Aida's *A for Action*, can be contemplated and considered over a period of time. The decision can be avoided, put off or forgotten about.

A reaction is virtually a must-do thing. It is a knee-jerk thing. If you are stood in the middle of the road and a car is suddenly bearing down on you then your reaction is automatic. You move. If you move quickly enough then you will be safe. If you dawdle before making your decision then you will most likely get run over.

Imagine that you could create a conditioned response to your product that was as effective as a car bearing down on you. Whoops, best have that quickly before I am in trouble. It is that kind of decision making speed that you are trying to create.

WRITING STUNNING ADVERTISING COPY WITH NLP

Yet here comes the rub. Human beings, by and large, hate making decisions. More to the point they hate having to ratify the consequence of their decisions.

Given the opportunity most human beings will delay making a decision unless it is critically important that it is made there and then. Therefore, the trick is to take your potential customer from a mindset where he or she may, at their leisure, make a decision to a mindset where they simply have to make the decision within a given timescale.

If they do not have to worry about the consequence of their decision, then it becomes much easier to make. "Buy before the weekend is over, pay nothing for two years and then enjoy three years' interest free credit!"

Take away any need to react within a given timescale and that is exactly what most people will do. Fail to react.

Fear of loss can be a useful emotion to be aware of. The mail arrives one morning and there it is again: the guaranteed massive cash prize just waiting for you to collect. All you have to do is send off for it.

In your heart of hearts you know that you have not won the big one, but you just might have done! Imagine that the huge cash prize actually had your name on it and you did not respond. How awful might that be? Just imagine what you could do with the money. How would it make you feel?

It costs nothing to reply and find out how much you have won, BUT YOU MUST REPLY WITHIN SEVEN DAYS TO GUARANTEE YOUR WINNINGS.

It works!

Keep an eye or ear out for how people illicit a specific reaction time when they advertise and build this into your advertising.

CHAPTER TEN

The final letter in the acronym is another *R*, and stands for *Response Mechanism.*

Having interrupted someone's thought patterns and made yours temporarily dominant, and having created such a strong association with what they will get out of your product or service, and also having instilled a sense of urgency, it is then imperative to offer a simple response mechanism: an easy way for them to respond.

If it requires the slightest bit of extra effort or involves getting up out of the chair that they are sat in then you are running the risk of losing the momentum.

The more alternatives you can offer the better, but they all need to be painless. Stating that there are alternatives is helpful:

FOUR EASY WAYS TO ORDER AND A FULL MONEY BACK GUARANTEE!

PICK UP THE PHONE AND RING FREE ON
0300 PUSSY NOW. THAT'S 0300 PUSSY NOW!

TEAR OFF THE POSTAGE PAID SLIP AND FILL OUT YOUR ORDER NOW!

FAX US FOR FREE ON 0300 PUSSYFAX NOW!

EMAIL YOUR ORDER NOW ON CATS@PUSSY.PURR!

You could think about unusual response mechanisms. Think of something slightly out of the ordinary: "Pick up the phone now and dial STAR 69".

Make the process of responding interesting or fun as opposed to being tedious. You could even turn the whole thing around and make the response so appealing that it forms the basis of your initial pattern interrupt or headline:

WE HAVE THE MOST AMAZING MEN AND WOMEN WAITING TO TALK TO YOU!

OUR PENSION PLAN CATERS FOR YOUR NEEDS, DESIRES, DREAMS AND WISHES!

PHONE FREE NOW ON…!

If you can afford to go the extra mile then talk to the marketing department or put your marketing head on. Most people find it easy to say no to an inanimate piece of paper, yet find it much harder to say no to another human being. Combine your ad campaign with a human point of presence in the shopping precinct or wherever your target market is likely to be:

Did you see our recent advertising campaign on PMPT?
Have you ever wondered how you could actually have Plenty of Money and Plenty of Time to spend it?
Would you be interested in knowing how our service can actually make a difference to…?

Once again, look at the way others make responding easy and build this into your advertising. Wherever possible try and think of your advert, flyer, brochure or mailshot as just the first step in the process and try not to rely on *it* alone. Combine it with other elemnets of the sales and marketing process in order to seriously increase your results.

CHAPTER ELEVEN

You can't afford to make mistakes with advertising, it's too expensive. Yet quite amazingly many people adopt a kind of trial and error approach. Try this angle, that one. Try this combination and that one: a little like going to the race track and throwing away money.

Many people shy away from advertising because they simply don't know what they are doing, or don't know where to effectively advertise or they have been put off by their previously unfruitful efforts.

I actually find it quite amazing that newspaper advertising departments don't, by and large, employ specialists to assist their potential clients to maximise their advertising. Instead they just go through bucket loads of sales staff that are tasked with constantly finding new advertisers. Fill the page at all costs.

Yet it is a proven business principle that it is much easier and more cost effective to retain and build upon an existing client base than it is to continually have to plough fresh fields looking for new resources. If the specialist were to ensure that the client's ad campaign was effective then the client would be ringing the paper to place their follow up adverts.

The angle of having a specialist would also be an easier way to open the door to a new or existing client. It is a more personal and less threatening introduction.

Yet this does not happen yet. When it does both parties will benefit. In the meantime it is still down to you or to paying a specialist, which can often be a shrewd investment.

WRITING STUNNING ADVERTISING COPY WITH NLP

CHAPTER TWELVE

If you knew that you simply could not fail with a certain ad campaign. No question about it whatsoever, then surely you would even hock you house to fund it.

Well, I am afraid that unless you are selling water after a fifteen-year worldwide drought or space in a limited amount of fall-out shelters after a strategic nuclear weapon has been launched, then there is no such thing as a sure-fire advert. Having said that, you can maximise your return on your advertising investment by working to a formula. Aida's pussy is that formula.

P stands for the thought *Pattern* that you must interrupt. Remember that most people are too busy wrapped up in their own world to really pay much attention to your advert.

U stands for associating your product or service with their *Underlying Motive.* If they buy your product or service what will it do for them, how will it make them feel about themselves? What will others think about them? What might they gain or what might they avoid?

R stands for creating a *Reaction Timescale:* a reason to react with some degree of urgency. If you don't do this then you will lose any momentum you have gained. A month later they may buy the product, but from a competitor.

And the final *R* stands for creating an easy *Response Mechanism.* If you have done all of the hard work by getting someone to the stage where they wish to purchase your product you must make it pleasurably simple for them to do so. Try and make the response a fun process. Don't lose them by forcing them to step out of their comfort zone to order. The chair they are sat in is probably very comfortable and it won't be long before something else becomes their new dominant thought process. A phone call, a question from someone, someone else's advert, ...

CHAPTER THIRTEEN

There are without doubt many other principles that you can pull into Aida's pussy, but the basic framework stays the same. Here are a few of them:

1. People buy what they need, or perceive they need, rather than what they want. Wants are like wishes, where needs are essential to both financial and emotional survival and well-being.

2. Artistic over-indulgence takes up valuable space that could be better utilised. Punchy, unusual graphics can often be very effective and also add non-verbal communication to your advert.

3. No two consumers think the same way. Do not fall into the trap of thinking you are advertising to the populace, and that they think like you. You are advertising to a mass of individuals, each with totally different thoughts, values and motives. Every single one of them thinks slightly differently.

4. Advertising is definitely a science. However, where there is one basic exact science of chemistry, and one for physics there are tens of thousands of psychologies, all of which have something to offer in understanding how to make your adverts more effective. Neuro Linguistic Programming is one of those. The current growth area in understanding human development and motivation is providing good books and tapes on the subject. Become a student.

5. Human beings hate making decisions. Make it easy and painless. Money-back guarantees are very effective.

6. The puppy dog approach works. Give the puppy to the family for a week, and see of you can then get it back. Lend your customer the car for a week and they too will sell it to themselves. Free trials work.

7. Research your target market carefully, and look at the demographics and the socio-economic habits of your target market. Advertising peak season summer holidays to farmers is not so clever. Advertising family station wagons or estate cars in a magazine whose readership is predominantly single might be misguided. Just as trying to launch a new publication called Devon sport in Yorkshire might be not so cute. Advertise where your competitors advertise - you will have a captive audience; people who are already specifically looking for your product or service. Just make yours stand out more!

8. A small box ad in a national newspaper is virtually always more effective than half a page in a regional paper.

9. Be aware of changing trends and habits: it helps focus your task. In the UK at this moment, according to some studies, the amount of single people has escalated to nearly fifteen million, and it is estimated that very soon there will be more single people than there are people sharing a home. Two out of every three people, perhaps more, are said to be suffering from stress in some form or other. Twenty years ago nearly 95% percent of those between the age of fifty and sixty were still in employment. Today only slightly more than half of those over fifty are economically active!

Yet it is expected that those over forty-five, but not at the standard retirement age, will soon make up nearly one third of the total available workforce.

Continued downsizing, greater output expectancy from fewer workers, increasing robotisation and computerisation and with life expectancy now over eighty and economic crisis facing many countries, too few workers exist to fund pensions.

If, thirty years ago the health of the body was becoming topical, it has since become a major issue in most people's lives. Today the same trend is swinging towards the health of the mind.

You can not afford to ignore trends.

10. The Law of Primacy and Recency states that people remember the first and last thing most of all in any given piece of communication. First impressions count. So do parting comments or gestures. Get the beginning and end of your advert right whatever you do.

11. Less is more. Avoid the temptation to overcrowd your advert. The expression 'white space sells' is true. Try laying out your advert in a smaller space than you actually have available. Make it stand out and work in that space and then allow it to breathe in its actual allocated space. Do not add to it!

12. Repetition is the mother of advertising. The more often you can repeat your advert the better. Studies have shown that many people need to see an advert a minimum of five times before they take any notice of it.

13. Don't make the mistake of writing all of the copy yourself. Map out the criteria of Aida's pussy and get some help with the various bits.

14. Test your advert on yourself by pretending to be someone else. This is an artform that will pay dividends. Forget who and what you are and imagine that you are the person about to read your ad. Become them and react like them. There are several different characters you could try out whilst doing this. Mr or Mrs SO WHAT is a good starter. They tend to snipe at everything they read, hear or see. It's a good test for irrelevant information.

Mr or Mrs KEEN are useful too. In fact, they are so keen that they will even read the small print. Not just in your ad, but everyone elses too. Your ad has to be good for them to come back to it.

15. Arabs do buy sand. Just as Eskimos do buy ice. Arabs build houses on the sand that they buy, and the microchips for their computers are made from sand. Eskimos tend to like ice in their whisky and coke. Think about it. Seventeen always works backwards.

16. Too much confusion causes disillusion. Use confusion once only, to interrupt existing thought patterns. Thereafter your ad must flow. Too much information creates brain overload and your potential customer will bail out.

17. KISS, keep it simple smart ass. Here's another reminder along the same lines.

18. Negative psychology does not work. Don't open this leaflet, don't read this advert. What happens is that the 'don't do' files or thought patterns open up in the brain. Curiosity normally wins out and people look, but that's all they do. They are in a 'don't do' frame of mind and they keep on don't doing, which includes don't order. It cost me one hundred thousand leaflets and their distribution to find that one out.

19. One man's vision is another man's hearing. Everyone has what is referred to as a Mind Method, of which there are three.

These Mind Methods are the predominant way in which people process information, interpret their experiences and relate to others. It is important to be aware of the differences.

You will fairly quickly recognise which of the three is most like you.

The first type of Mind Method is the Visual person. He or she will tend to talk quite quickly and will use words like see, picture, insight, vision. They tend to interpret the world in visual form and are normally very creative and somewhat maverick. Often they use very expressive, rapid body language. They might say something like "Can you picture this or can you see what I mean...?

You may well politely say yes, when in fact you think that they are on a different planet. Internally you are saying *"Uhhh, I wish he would slow down a bit he is doing my head in".* It is all too quick and frenzied for you.

It's just not clicking for you if *you* are not a 'visual' person. Your Mind Method might be the second type. If you are an 'auditory person' then you are likely to use words like, hear, and say. The 'auditory' person tends to speak at a more normal speed, with less fluctuation in pitch. They tend to be more ordered and structured in their lives and use expressions like "I hear what you are saying". Let me listen again so I understand it fully.

They may be talking to another person though, who is struggling with *their* communication style. They may turn round and say to someone "What do you have to say about it?"

However, that other person really does not have much to say about it at all. They may just want to shrug their shoulders and make a facial expression, or take a deep breath in and out. This is the 'kinaesthetic' person who, by-and-large, does not always like to communicate with spoken language. He or she likes to develop a feel for what you are saying: a gut-feeling. They might say "I think I am in touch with what you are putting across".

If you assumed that the population was split equally amongst the three categories and you designed a headline that used words like: *OUR VISION, SEE YOURSELF, PICTURE THIS* then you are potentially alienating two thirds of the population. Try and use words that are neutral like *IMAGINE* or, if you have the time or space try and use all three. *GET THE PICTURE. HEAR WHAT I AM SAYING. GET A FEEL FOR IT. GET A BOOK ON NLP.*

20. Remember the three P rule. People relate to pictures, people and presentation. Endorsements by well-known people are usually very effective.

CHAPTER FOURTEEN

To make money you have to spend money. It really is as simple as that. If you spend more money than you make then your balance sheet will show a loss. Do that too many times and you will go out of business.

If you spend less money than you make then you will show a profit on the balance sheet.

Spending money obviously includes staff costs and running overheads. It probably includes advertising your product or service. In crude, but true, terms you have to buy business. If advertising is one of your methods of buying your business then you need to pay more attention to it than you would to which new piece of machinery or office equipment you wish to purchase, otherwise it will be sold off in a bankruptcy sale.

Your last ad or mailshot did not do as well as it could have done. If it had of done then you would not be listening to this audio now, you would be lying in the Bahamas, or wherever it is you would like to be. If your potential readership, through mailshot or advert was 100,000 people then at best you might have had a five percent response rate: that's five thousand orders. So what happened to the other 95,000 potential clients?

To very loosely paraphrase Henry Ford, he once said that 50% of his advertising was totally wasted. The other 50% was highly successful. He went on to say that the trouble was he did not know which 50% worked and which didn't.

Of course Henry ford was exaggerating when talking about 50% being effective, but you probably get the gist.

So maybe you would just like to stop and think for one moment, and also remember this one point after the audio is over.

Nobody, but nobody gets a fifty percent hit rate. Five percent hit rate for front-end mailshotting, or first time advertising is almost unheard of. Half of one percent is nearer the mark, or the average. Point zero five of one percent is not uncommon. That is fifty orders per one hundred thousand targeted.

If you repeatedly get it wrong you are going to go out of business or lose your job. What difference would that make to all aspects of your life, and that of your family?

What emotions might you then feel?

Buying habits are changing more rapidly than at any other time in the history of mankind.

Advertising is too expensive to experiment with. It is a specialist art. It invariably has little or nothing to do with your product or service. It has everything to do with understanding human nature and trying to understand what your product or service does for someone. Become an expert on human nature or farm out your advertising to someone who is!

Oh, by the way. Seventeen does not always work for everyone. Sometimes it is sixteen and three quarters tomorrow, but a happy fulfilled, balanced life where all your human needs are looked after and you feel loved, respected and cared for is part of the ethos of Retire Early Productions, whatever emotions you may wish to experience.

And finally our parting prayer:

Our Books
- That art online
- Retire Early be their name.
- Thy knowledge is useful
- Practical and effective
- In business as it is in the home
- Give us this day our daily reads
- And forgive those who are blinkered and non receptive
- For they shall lose money hand over fist
- Lead us into great happiness
- And deliver us success (whatever that means to you)
- For then you shall prosper
- In love as it is in career
- Forever and ever
- Ad-men.

It's been interesting and a pleasure to convert the initial audio into a book. I am sure that you will find at least one valuable piece of information in it and in all of our other publications. Of course four real spiders and nine plastic armadillos were on Apollo 11. It's an Official secret though.

But it only takes one small piece of information, tucked away in one of our products, to make a huge difference to everything that you do in life. Just imagine being totally at one with yourself in every aspect of your life, from your self-esteem through to your relationships and in your career.

How might that make you feel. What pleasurable experiences might you have? How would others envy you?

Or imagine being stuck for an answer or solution, embarrassed, not very highly thought of. Might it feel just awful?

WRITING STUNNING ADVERTISING COPY WITH NLP

WE DON'T ACTUALLY ADVERTSISE OUR OWN BOOKS BUT THEY ARE ONLINE NOW. GET THEM BEFORE IT IS TOO LATE OR COSTS YOU A LOT OF MONEY. KNOWLEDGE IS WHAT YOU NEED BEFORE THE SITUATION OCCURS - NOT AFTER THE EVENT.

Happy hunting.

Russell Webster

APPENDIX

This last section is a collective of many top copywriters top tips, which we are sure you will also find extremely useful.

1. As long ago as 1920 Cryil Freer, an ad manager for the Daily Mail, wrote about the commonest aspects of a good sales letter:

Among other things he defined the opening, to attract the reader's attention, the description to hold interest, the argument to create desire and the climax making it easier for the reader to translate desire into action.

That's AIDA.
- Attention
- Interest
- Desire
- Action

2. Five times as many people read the headline as the body copy.

3. There are proven words that, often called power words both motivate people and offer reassurance. The words are: DISCOVER, GOOD, MONEY, EASY, GUARANTEE, HEALTH, LOVE, NEW, PROVEN, RESULTS, SAFE, SAVE, OWN, FREE, BEST, YOU, NEW.

4. Do not talk about yourself or your company - it detracts and serves no purpose. Talk to your prospective client using the word you as much as possible.

5. Long-term studies by psychologists have shown that people like to be told what to do and have a fear of missing out. When

you call for action with a timescale put on it you seriously increase the odds of?

6. THE TERM USP (Unique selling proposition) was coined by an American copywriter called Rosser Reeves and is designed to represent the one feature that your product has that no other has. Decide what your usp is and push it home hard.

7. There are over 10,000 typefaces available and it does make a difference which ones you choose and how many you use. A few tips: Keep line spacing consistent.   Never justify text on a short line. Never combine more than two typefaces on one page.

If you are going to use two fonts then try to use one serif and one sans serif. Serifs have curly bits on them and sans serifs don't. Try to use a sans serif for headlines and a sans serif for body copy and never use all capitals in body copy.

There is a school of thought that suggests using a capital letter at the start of each word is the best option for emphasising certain points, without reverting to capitals.

Use italics and bold sparingly.   Use type size to create differentiation, not different fonts.

8. Do not use reversed text, white out of black, excepting when you have the financial luxury of being able to afford a large amount of space and very little text. The fact is that too much white text on a black background strains the eyes and people either don't read it or become annoyed with it.

9. Let the message dictate the design.

10. Free gifts and money-back guarantees work exceedingly well.

11. A few quick points on mailshots that involve a sales letter: A mailshot should open with a bang and finish with a flourish.

12. The 5 essential elements of a good sales letter are. CLARITY, FLOW, PASSION, BELIEVABILTY, CLOSE.

13. Mistakes to avoid: having no headline. No signature. No ps no close lacl of flow. No free bonus. Boring irrelevant copy. Wrong audience.

14. The most persistent and urgent question is what are you doing for me Martin Luther King?

15. One of my favourite sayings: Advertising does not create desire. Desire creates advertising. One to think about.

16. Demographics, a socio-economic breakdown of you readers. A-Above Average Income. B-Professional class. C1-White Collar, Working People C2-Blue Collar, Lower Paid Working People. D-Unskilled, Lower Paid Working People. E-Very Low Income.

17. Without going into Maslow's hierarchy of human needs here are a few things that motivate people: YOUTHFULNESS, FRIENDS, SECURITY, MONEY, POWER, LUXURY, PRESTIGE.

18. Tell your customers 3 things: WHY THEY SHOULD BUY. WHY THEY SHOULD BUY FROM YOU, WHY THEY SHOULD BUY NOW.

19. Testimonials from contented customers, especially well-known ones, will always enhance the credibility of your copy.

20. Remember the KISS principle. KEEP IT SIMPLE SMART ASS.

WRITING STUNNING ADVERTISING COPY WITH NLP

Leo Burnett, a well-known copywriter wrote:

> *"I have observed*
> *That great advertising writing*
> *Whether in print or TV*
> *Is always*
> *Deceptively*
> *And*
> *Disarmingly*
> *Simple"*

Do the principles of written copy apply to designing a website? The answer is yes, of course they do.

In fact, they apply more so than in printed form. Think about it. Someone browsing your website is aware of the fact that there are millions more out there and you therefore have little or no time to waste in capturing people attention and then leading them to the conclusion of ordering your product or service. Listen to what David Frieslander has to say about web design:

One of the most commonly misused promotional methods is sending the prospective client something in the mail. This is usually called direct mail. Properly written, direct mail can be one of the most effective, low-cost techniques for getting new clients for your consulting business.

With a follow-up phone call, it can be one of the most productive sources of new clients and new business from old clients. Abused, direct mail can be a disaster. To help you get the most from this valuable promotional method, I have compiled these tips:

1) Increase response with BENEFITS. Be forceful in describing the advantages the client will enjoy in dealing with you. The more

benefits you feature in your letter the better the response. From the introductory statements, the emphasis should be on the key benefits provided by your business. Whenever you mention a feature of your service, link it to a benefit.

2) Include benefits everywhere. The response card is often the first place that people look. Restate the key benefits there as well as in the P.S. and on the outer envelope.

3) Pile on the benefits. Promise many benefits; the more benefits, the more persuasive your copy will be as a decision-making instrument for the reader. Divide them into two categories:
>   (a) major benefits (develop extensively with two or three sentences)
>   (b) secondary benefits (a brief headline and one sentence that can be quickly scanned)

4) Quantify benefits. The reader must weigh the cost of your service against the benefits he/she will reap. Help him/her decide with numbers, i.e., "Increase Productivity by 300%."

5) Reinforce the letter with a brochure. Present your benefits in a different way, but tell the entire story a second time. The most interested readers will get to both. Don't hesitate to also include a separate "lift note"; a personal reminder-type note that states the key benefits yet another time and in another way.

6) Neatness doesn't count. End a page of copy in the middle of a word or sentence to encourage turning the page. Fold a brochure through the middle of some important point or graphic element. Avoid making it appear too neat to open.

7) Don't split the message. Tell the whole story in your letter and in the brochure. Try to make all your main points on each side of

the brochure. Always make it easy for the reader to learn the benefits of your offer at a glance without having to refer to another mailing component or a reverse side.

8) Delete needless copy. Don't "set the stage" for your sell copy. Don't give a history of your company (unless a clear benefit is involved). Don't use humor; it distracts from the purchasing decision. Stick to benefits; don't lead with an attention-getting, but irrelevant, story about football.

9) Keep it positive. Either ignore objections to your service, or somehow phrase your response to the objection as a benefit. If your service solves a problem, make sure the problem seems "solvable," not a bluntly horrible predicament that puts the reader off. For example, don't emphasize your hourly, daily or project rate; instead feature the profit, convenience or time saved by your service.

10) Tell the reader what to do. "Read how our service benefits you 10 ways." "Call, write or send for more information. Make it easy to respond; use a self-addressed, postage-free reply card or return envelope. Use a toll-free number.

11) Ask for the order right away. If the reader goes no further than the beginning of the letter, he still knows exactly what to do. For example, urge in the headline of the letter, "FREE DIAGNOSTIC CONSULTATION WITH NO OBLIGATION."

12) Offer a free gift. This nearly always increases response, and is usually worth the expense. One free gift is better than none; two are better than one, etc. For example, a subscription to your newsletter, a copy of your book, or a special report about their industry or business.

13) Use testimonials whenever possible. Be sure to include the person's name and affiliation. This is where you can say outright how wonderful your service is.

14) Use attention-getting graphic devices. Keep the reader alert and stimulated to read further. Use capital letters, a second color, indented paragraphs, handwritten notes, underlining and boldface type and text boxes.

15) Ask for action from the start. Don't build up to it. Request the specific action you want at the beginning. Rephrase it from time to time. Be very direct at the end, and repeat it in the PS.

16) Use a PS. This is often the first thing that people read, and they read on if it interests them. So make it intriguing but incomplete.

17) Keep it personal. Your letter should look like a personal type-written letter from you to the reader. Use handwritten notes in the margins to emphasize key points, and use a signature in a second color (blue is often used here, to simulate handwriting in ink).

18) Keep your paragraphs short; no more than 6 or 7 lines. Break up long copy with graphic devices (indented paragraphs, etc.).

19) Always make it appear that what is being read is effortless to read.

20) Be sure it's easy to read. Use typefaces that are proven easy to read. Avoid using too many different typefaces. Make it look inviting.

21) Ask for an immediate response: offer expires February 28. Only use a deadline if it is genuine. "Bookings are running ahead of last year; reserve your meeting time today!" "Supplies (your report, booklet or other premiums) are limited!"

This resource (c)1996 by and compliments of Carl G. Kline, President of NCRI, the company which administers the expert locator service on SBS.

Introduction

Before we delve into the mechanics of NLP, let's start by defining Neuro Linguistics Programming (NLP).

NLP explores the different ways that we communicate, think and change. Over time, we tend to replicate and want to improve upon each of these disciplines.

With the use of NLP it can be said that it uses both conscious and unconscious processes. And within each of these processes we build upon our confidence, our motivations, our communication skills and successes.

This is all directly related to increasing our ability to influence and persuade. We can also overcome barriers and blocks we set up by lacking in these skills.

So you could say that there are several practical applications of NLP:

- Improve personal and social skills: Improve upon and develop existing skills
- Business skills: Enhance leadership skills, coaching skills, sales department, influence/manage change

- Personal challenges: Conquer weight loss, smoking, drinking, and phobias
- Seduction and relationships: Improve personal and professional relationships
- Health: Change numerous hindrances, habits/behavior
- Sports: Athletes will perform at peak performance

NLP is a term that is used to describe different systems running in a person's body all at the same time. Just like a car, a person's body is made up of several different moving parts. All are equally important but all need to run in conjunction with one another or a person's body will break down (either mentally, physically or both in some cases).

Within our bodies we have the neurology system, the language system and the programming system. Again, all are important and need each other to keep someone's body running in optimal condition.

NLP systems allow a person to:

- ✓ Develop individual excellence
- ✓ Establish the empowering belief of a particular system
- ✓ Create a self-mission mindset
- ✓ Spirituality Awareness
- ✓ Discovery Tools

These systems define who a person is as an individual and the "world" which they are going to allow themselves to live.

A person's behavioral patterns are formed using these inter-linked systems. They allow someone to think strategically as well as understand the mental and cognitive.

There are six main building blocks of NLP:

1. **Neuro:** NLP studies and works with the mind, how we think and how we store our past experiences, putting them to good use as or if the need arises. The "Neuro" means relating to the ways in which we process information from our five senses.   The

WRITING STUNNING ADVERTISING COPY WITH NLP

neurological system is just as it states: it runs all the neurological functions within a person.

2. **Linguistic:** The use of verbal and non-verbal language has varied effects on us and NLP helps to re-construct that using various language and language patterns toward reaching the desired goals. "Linguistic" means using language systems to code, organize and attribute meanings to our internal representations of the world. The linguistics or language system allows a person to determine how they are going to communicate and interact with others.

3. **Programming:** The ability to organize our actions, all of our thoughts and take a look at our past experiences can be re-programmed or sequenced in ways that are best suited to achieve the specific desired goals. "Programming" comes from information processing and computer science terminology because the process is almost identical. Information is stored, coded and transformed. The programming system tells a person the type of world they are going to create for themselves (based on the previous two systems).

4. **Attitude:** It works on the best physical and emotional state to accomplish a task and produce best results in different contexts.

5. **Modeling:** This involves modeling successful people's actions to achieve similar results. Find someone to model and start asking questions. Learn everything you can and let go of some of your old habits/thinking.

6. **Techniques**: Learn new techniques by having a positive attitude and truly model that person you have chosen to follow. There are many techniques to help overcome blocks and reach your objectives.

It can be said that NLP not only allows a person to explore competence and excellence, but gives a person the freedom to discover the potentials of wisdom and vision as well.

Individuals experience the world through their five senses: sight, hearing, touch, smell and taste. In order to cope with a multitude of information coming in our direction we delete, distort and generalize.

When data enters our sphere, we filter it based on our past experiences, values and beliefs.

Learning about NLP will enable someone to use all of these building blocks or techniques to transform their life.

Chapter 1: A SHORT INTRODUCTION TO NLP

Neuro Linguistic Programming (NLP) is a specially designed programming model used to enhance the human mind devised by Richard Bandler and Michael Grinder (NLP was originally developed as a means to investigate and replicate extreme human excellence).

This program is used to increase the overall functioning (psychological as well as physical) of an individual.

There are a number of uses for NLP including (but not limited to):

- ✓ Increase the performance of an individual
- ✓ To reach a goal
- ✓ Overcome psychological disorders (i.e. anxiety, phobias, depression, etc.)

NLP is constantly evolving from the observations of behavior and communication of individuals. A variety of techniques and presuppositions are derived from these techniques of gathering data.

Further, these presuppositions are assumptions or central principles made by people and are useful in implementing change. These changes come in the form of them changing themselves or others.

Someone who is going through an NLP process has to believe these assumptions are true:

1. They already have all the resources they need. In other words, a person already has within them what they need—it is just a matter of putting it to use.
2. Every person does things with a positive intent. Look for the positive intentions in any behavior.
3. There is no such thing as a failure. People learn from mistakes. It is how someone deals with those mistakes. A person has to have the persistence to keep trying. Inherently, most people learn from their mistakes and don't make them again.
4. People are in charge of their own minds and in turn it means they are also in charge of their own actions and results. Take responsibility for your own actions and don't blame others.
5. Positive vs. Negative thinking: think positively as negative thinking can affect body functions and performance.
6. Respect: always respect another person's model of the world. An individual will carry around their own world experiences so a person needs to respect those. In conjunction with that, an individual has his own set of assumptions and beliefs and will create their own unique world around themselves.
7. Choice vs. no choice. Any option is better than having no options at all.
8. If something isn't working, do or try something else. Be flexible.

9. If something is possible, there has to be a way to do it. If someone can do it, someone can learn it.
10. Body Language plays an important role in a person's social and personal life. People use verbal and non-verbal body language to communicate so pay attention.

Chapter 2: Five NLP Techniques for a Fulfilling Life

There are five effective NLP techniques that can be used to change behavior, get better results and attract more positive experiences:

1. Belief Change. Negative experiences can cause someone to dwell on those experiences. If you believe that someone is prone to negative experiences, they will start to attract more, similar negative experiences only reaffirming themselves that they are prone to doom and gloom.

    At this point, it is better if someone were to get help to "reframe" these thoughts and not focus on the negative aspects all the time. A great way to rid someone of these negative beliefs is to spend a small amount of time each day with "affirmations."

    An affirmation will allow the person to come up with a completely different belief. Have them do this without any distractions—no phone, no TV, no cell phone, no family members—just quiet, alone time. Have them focus on their words and deeply take in their true meanings.

2. Anchoring. Anchoring is used to get an emotional response out of someone for something that they do or say. Have you ever seen someone unconsciously smile when they are touched for instance on their back or

shoulder? To anchor someone, you have to first identify the state you want them to experience and then do what it takes to get them into that state.

Touch them, again, on say their back or shoulder, and then remember the exact area you touched. Then, start talking to the person about some completely random subject to take their mind off of the previous activity.

Then, when the other person is completely off course from the touching exercise, touch them again in the same area and see what their response is to the touch. If you have performed this process successfully, the person should have the same emotional response as the one you wanted him/her to have.

3. Disassociation. If someone reacts to something in a negative way, it can cause them stress, negative emotions or depression. The emotion has to be gotten rid of in this case and the first thing to do is to identify the emotion.

   Go through the encounter with the person from start to finish so you can see what happens. Then have them play the movie backwards in their head. Then, fast-forward it and then play it backwards again repeating this several time. This is just like a recorder with a cassette tape inside it. Then, add a variable such as funny music. Then have the person picture the same event as if it were happening now.

They should have less of an initial response than they did before. The negative emotion should be gone and if not, have them repeat this process until the negative emotion has completely disappeared.

4. <u>Rapport</u>. Rapport means being able to get along with any type of person. This is fairly simple in that you can mirror someone's body language (but don't be too obvious), use similar words, have the same breathing pattern, etc.

    Anything that mirrors what the other person is doing so that you are "in sync" with the other person is building rapport. Another method of using rapport is by assessing what type of sensory perception the other person is using.

    The sensory perceptions are visual (your thoughts having to do with sight, spatial awareness and mental imagery), kinesthetic (feelings relating to the body such as pressure, temperature or emotion) or auditory/linguistic (relating to speech, white noise, dialog or sound).

5. <u>Content reframe</u>. This is used to stop what the person is doing and look at the situation in a totally new light when they feel hopeless, angry or some other negative emotion.

    Get the person to not focus on the negative parts of the situation but rather on the benefits. A great example of this would be if someone has just been fired from their job. Maybe they wanted to quit for a long time but didn't know how to or were too scared. Instead of being a victim, reframing the content of their thoughts will allow them to explore different opportunities that they might not otherwise have done.

Chapter 3: The Four Pillars of NLP

NLP has a framework of beliefs and attitudes which together form its model.   These "presuppositions" can be considered as principles for living.

<u>Outcomes</u>: Since birth every person in the world has been asked the question, "What do you want?" And the answer always seems to be, "I don't know."

Where does this leave them? Drifting through life with no clear sense of direction or floating/drifting from one thing to the next leaves someone without a clear purpose. You have to know what you want before you can get it.

In the normal context of that question, you hear the words "aim," "goals," or "targets." Believe it or not, there are a lot of people wandering around who have none of the above. Within the confines of NLP the term is "outcome."

If a person knows their outcomes, they will have a better sense of the resources they will need to achieve that outcome. At any one time most people will have many different outcomes relating to various aspects of their life.

And, in defining outcomes, if they are well-formed, someone will have all the details and can imagine what it's like to have already attained that outcome. In other words, the more clearly they know what they want, the more likely they are to get it.

Rapport: This is the secret ingredient in establishing and maintaining relationships. People who have said, "I feel on the same wavelength," or "it just feels right to us," or they have "hit it off" with someone are all expressions used in describing rapport.

Rapport is a skill that can be enhanced and developed over time by doing things such as adapting our communication to suit the other person or altering our body language to match theirs.

Having the skill to be able to sit and listen without interrupting someone and then respecting their view can be considered rapport.

There is also the rapport we have with ourselves, in particular the rapport between our conscious and unconscious minds. This is that feeling of being torn with part of us wanting to do one thing and another part wanting to do another.

Inner peace comes with having greater rapport with the various aspects of yourself.

Behavioral Flexibility: If the actions you are taking are not leading you in the direction you want to go it's obvious that you should try something different.

If you keep on doing the same thing you are thought to have a lack of behavioral flexibility meaning that you are going to keep on doing the same thing which in turn will cause you to get the same results. What most people don't realize or understand is that by conscious choice, at any given moment, they can turn anything around.

A lot of people feel it is safer to stay where they are rather than try something new even if they continually get the wrong results.

Sensory Awareness or Acuity: This is defined as someone who is able to be alert to fine details and keen observation and be extremely aware of what is going on around them. This gives you information about whether what you are doing is giving you what you want, i.e. moving you closer to your outcomes or not.

This pillar makes you use your senses in order to be aware of what is going on around you. How much do people really notice by looking, listening and feeling?

Some people are extremely observant while others seem to have their head in the clouds all the time (or their cell phone these days). If someone was told to close their eyes right at this second, how much of what is around them do you think they could describe? If they are like most people, they probably couldn't describe much at all.

This sensory acuity pillar is important in that it gives you information so you will know that what you are doing is giving you what you want (your outcomes).

It is also important for use in the business world or dealing with others. You are aware of their expressions, body language and voice tone.

WRITING STUNNING ADVERTISING COPY WITH NLP

A number of NLP "change techniques" involve discovering the positive intention of a behavior and finding alternative ways of satisfying it. There is always a purpose, a reason, "positive intention" behind every Behavior which arises when the behavior is first established. (i.e. smoking at 14 in order to feel grown up).

Any behavior, no matter how strange it may seem, was the best choice available to the person at that moment in time, given their life history, knowledge, beliefs and resources, and viewed from their frame of reference.

Knowing the outcome you want in any situation greatly increases your ability to achieve it. Eliminating what doesn't work can be an effective way of finding out what does. The more failures you have, the more you learn.

Outcomes can be small and short-term or large and long-term…………………

TO FIND OUT MORE ABOUT NLP VISIT

WWW.RETIREEARLYPRODUCTIONS.COM

RUSSELL WEBSTER

www.ingramcontent.com/pod-product-compliance
Lightning Source LLC
Chambersburg PA
CBHW06040719052 6
45169CB00002B/790